Original title:
Life's Answers Are Written in the Stars

Copyright © 2025 Creative Arts Management OÜ
All rights reserved.

Author: Rosalie Bradford
ISBN HARDBACK: 978-1-80566-144-3
ISBN PAPERBACK: 978-1-80566-439-0

Messages from the Milky Way

In the sky, the jokes are high,
Twinkling lights that wink and sigh.
Comets chuckle, meteors tease,
While planets spin with cosmic ease.

The moon pulls pranks on ocean tides,
Whispering secrets where humor hides.
Stars play cards; oh, what a sight!
Laughing louder through the night.

Celestial Maps and Forgotten Dreams

Maps of stars, drawn with flair,
Charting dreams from here to there.
Constellations point and giggle,
As they weave and dance, they wiggle.

Forgotten wishes ride the breeze,
As shooting stars bring giggling ease.
We laugh aloud, the cosmos sways,
In this circus of endless rays.

The Language of Stardust

Stardust speaks in playful tones,
Mixing laughter with ancient bones.
Galaxies chuckle, swirling on high,
In the night, they whisper and sigh.

Aliens chuckle at our concerns,
With every blink, a new joke churns.
They send us hints from far and wide,
While we're here, caught in our pride.

Navigating Tomorrow's Skies

With navigation charts astray,
Tomorrow's skies lead us away.
Stars throw parties, we can't find,
The vibes are cosmic, oh so kind.

Spaceships zoom, but we hold tight,
As nebulas giggle, shining bright.
In this celestial ride we trust,
With laughter's spark, it's a must.

Signs in the Cosmic Veil

Twinkling lights in the night sky,
They whisper secrets as they fly.
If you squint hard, you might just see,
A dancing comet saying, "Join me!"

The planets gossip with their spins,
Telling tales of forgotten sins.
Mars argues with a stubborn star,
While Venus laughs, saying, "How bizarre!"

A Map of Light in Darkness

When midnight strikes, the stars align,
A cosmic map with silly signs.
Follow Orion's belt, oh please,
But watch out for those pesky bees!

A big dipper spills its drink,
While little stars just stop to blink.
If you squint, no need to mope,
You might just find a cosmic soap!

Dreaming Under a Canopy of Stars

Lying back on the grass so green,
I chat with the moon, who's quite the queen.
She tells me jokes about comet tails,
And how to dodge the galactic snails!

Clouds join in, pulling stars apart,
Making funny shapes—it's a work of art.
I laugh so hard, I start to swirl,
As stars play tag, giving them a twirl!

The Glittering Codex Above

Above my head, a book of dreams,
Filled with goofy cosmic themes.
The starry pages flip and glow,
As Saturn winks, says, "Check me out, bro!"

Galaxies dance, swirling in glee,
While asteroids sip their cosmic tea.
In this bright codex, laughter reigns,
As stars tell tales of their silly trains!

The Whispering Universe

At night, the stars start to chat,
With jokes that make you laugh and splat.
They giggle and snicker, quite a sight,
While we ponder our snacks, feeling light.

Constellations play as cosmic jesters,
Winking at earthlings like sly investors.
They tell us secrets in astral delight,
Like, "Balance your accounts, or take a flight!"

Fragments of Time in Starlight

Fragments of time flicker above,
Each a silly whisper of cosmic love.
The Milky Way's a slippery slide,
Where comets race and nebulae hide.

They say, "Look sharp, and catch a drift!"
But mostly they just give you a lift.
A guide to laughter in the night's dome,
Making distance feel like a cozy home.

The Odyssey of Celestial Voices

Join the stars on a rollicking spree,
Where they plot to pull pranks, just wait and see!
Galaxies bursting with giggles in tow,
While meteors swoosh with a comical glow.

"Why did the asteroid cross the lane?"
One twinkles bright, "To avoid the reign!"
Oh, cosmic buddies with their tricks and schemes,
Have us chuckling loud in our wildest dreams.

Eternal Echoes of the Cosmos

Eternal echoes bounce off the night,
Sounding like laughter mixed with slight fright.
"Yo, planets! How's the vibe up there?"
"Pretty stellar, just hanging in the air!"

Voices from Saturn give funny replies,
"Try these rings, they're a hit for the pies!"
It's a cosmic party, where we all belong,
Dancing amidst nebulae, holding strong.

The Astral Oracle Speaks

Oh, the cosmos talks in whispers light,
Ask a question, behold your insight!
A comet giggles, a planet winks,
In this celestial chat, only humor links.

Stars may clash, they dance like jesters,
Good vibes from Mars, and weird ones from jesters.
Asteroids laugh as they pass on by,
Gravity's humor? It'll lift you high!

Constellations plot as if in a play,
Witness their antics by night or by day.
As you search for truths up in the bright skies,
Remember to chuckle, wisdom wears a disguise!

So if you feel lost, just look above,
Find the starlight shining, oh how they shove!
They'll tickle your thoughts, amidst cosmic cheer,
In the tapestry of space, all laughs are clear!

Among the Celestial Bodies

In the vastness, where planets spin round,
Oddball orbits make the cosmic sound.
Venus is sassy, with style and flair,
While Uranus chuckles, with something to share.

Jupiter's storm, a swirling delight,
Could it be laughter, or a meteor fright?
Saturn rings in with some flair of its own,
Wishes on comets? Just a pilot flown!

Amongst the stars, it's a wild goose chase,
Nebulas giggle, in their colorful grace.
Galaxy clusters having a grand tea,
Cosmic gossip flies, over cups of stardust spree!

So spin in your chair, let your worries unfurl,
The universe's tales will make your heart twirl.
For in this grand dance, with stars as your friends,
You'll find that the fun in space never ends!

Messages from the Milky Way

The Milky Way writes, in a whimsical style,
With chocolatey stars that stretch every mile.
Galactic secrets, all wrapped in a jest,
Look out for a supernova dressed in a vest!

Black holes are the comedians of night,
Sucking up light with sheer delight.
While shooting stars race like they've got a bet,
In this cosmic comedy, no one gets wet!

Pulsars bleep in their rhythmic dance,
Sending signals to the stars with a wink and a glance.
In this spiral of laughter, effortlessly spun,
You'll realize the cosmos is far from done!

So wave to the planets, twirl with the moons,
In the bizarre universe, we'll all be buffoons.
Keep your eyes skyward, embrace the array,
For joy is the message from the Milky Way!

The Universe's Silent Language

In silence, the stars scribble tales untold,
With giggles and whispers, secrets unfold.
A wink from the moon, a nudge from the sun,
In this non-verbal chat, it's all just for fun!

Planets play charades, dodging asteroids,
While meteors race, making noise like noids.
Interstellar banter, in twinkling bright light,
For humor's the glue that keeps laughter in flight.

Galactic giggles echo through the void,
Every supernova, a punchline deployed.
When you hear the silence, lean in close,
The universe laughs, let's raise a toast!

So dance among stars, laugh at the skies,
In this cosmic circus, joy never dies.
For the universe speaks, with humor and charm,
In the silent language, there's no need for alarm!

The Silent Symphony of the Stars

In the late-night sky, I found some news,
A million twinkling lights, wearing shiny shoes.
They dance in silence, a cosmic delight,
While I chase my socks in the moon's silver light.

Orion's belt's just a fancy disguise,
He's really just holding up his pants, oh, the lies!
While Sirius winks, and all others clap,
The universe giggles, as I take a nap.

Leo's roaring? Nah, just a sneeze,
The stars light up when they feel the breeze.
Galaxies grin at our earthly fuss,
As I trip on my dog, and he gives a cuss.

So next time you gaze and ponder the night,
Just laugh with the cosmos, hold your dreams tight.
For in the starlit canvas, there's humor so bright,
Even the Milky Way's just a cosmic bite!

Patterns in the Celestial Tapestry.

Pleiades giggles, all stars in a row,
Playing hide and seek, as the comet's too slow.
They wear twinkling capes, quite the fashion scene,
While I search for my keys, in all that I glean.

In the void's great expanse, I hear a loud snore,
Is that Big Dipper dreaming, or wanting one more?
With stardust and laughter, they twirl in the gale,
As I ponder my lunch, should it be pizza or kale?

The constellations chuckle, weaving their tales,
Of fierce meteor showers and whimsical gales.
And as I trip over my cat in the dark,
The heavens explode into giggles and sparks.

So raise your eyes high, let the chuckles cascade,
For up there, the universe throws a grand parade.
Just follow their lead, join the cosmic dance,
And maybe, just maybe, you'll find a new chance!

Celestial Whispers

The Moon told the Sun, 'You glow way too bright,'
He winked back and said, 'I just light up the night!'
While Jupiter's jamming with all of its moons,
I hum my own tune, extracting some spoons.

Stars whisper secrets only late at night,
Like how Mars lost its hat in a tumble of flight.
They laugh at my worries, 'Oh, isn't he cute?'
As I chase my own shadow, in search of my loot.

The comets swirl past, with a wink and a fly,
They wink and they giggle, oh why oh why?
As I ponder the questions of why it's so tough,
They play games in the twilight, as I huff and puff.

So join in the chatter of cosmic delight,
For the universe knows things are always all right.
Embrace every chuckle, each giggle, each star,
And live for the laughter, wherever you are!

Beyond the Horizon of Dreams

As night blankets all, we look up and see,
A sky full of wonders and whimsy, oh me!
The stars throw a party for those feeling blue,
With drinks made of stardust and a cosmic stew.

I asked the Milky Way for a sip of its wine,
It said, 'Sorry, my friend, we're on starry design.'
While Saturn's rings twirl like a dance at the prom,
I trip over gravity, but still stay calm.

The planets are gossiping, sharing their tales,
Of space-time adventures, and interstellar fails.
And just as I ponder my place in this scheme,
The cosmos erupts, 'It's all just a dream!'

So float in your thoughts beyond horizons that gleam,
For laughter and joy are the glue of our team.
With every star shining, our worries take flight,
Let's twirl with the cosmos, and join in tonight!

Whispers Between the Galaxies

In cosmic jest, the planets play,
They spin and twirl, in a wobbly way.
A comet sneezes, a supernova laughs,
While asteroids take silly photographs.

A black hole grumbles, demanding more snacks,
While stardust giggles, snuggled between cracks.
The universe winks, with glittery grace,
As meteors dance in a starry embrace.

Starry Conversations in the Dark

In twilight talks, when shadows creep,
Stars share secrets, a cosmic leap.
The moon tells jokes, and they're quite a hit,
About planets that trip—oh, what a skit!

Asteroids gossip, with comets aflame,
While aliens chuckle, all in the game.
Galaxies shuffle, with laughter they sway,
Echoing humor through night's vast array.

The Infinite Atlas of Dreams

A map of wishes drawn in light,
With ticklish stars that shine so bright.
Nebulas make funny faces at best,
Creating smiles in the cosmic jest.

Black holes hiding, where did they go?
They're off playing hide and seek, you know!
The universe giggles, as dreams supply,
A comet's confetti, dancing on high.

Celestial Clues in the Silhouette

In shadows they whisper, the stars conspire,
Plotting pranks on those who inquire.
The constellations argue, who's the best?
While shooting stars zip by, full of zest.

They wink at the earthlings, with cheeky delight,
Hoping for laughs in the still of the night.
As the cosmos chuckles, it's hard to see,
That the best kind of wisdom is pure comedy.

Tides of Cosmic Wisdom

In the sky, a pizza floats,
With cheese like the full moon's glow.
Martians munching, oh what jests,
As gravity's pulling, they say hello.

A comet's tail wags, quite a tease,
While planets spin with joyful glee.
Asteroids dance, if you please,
In cosmic chaos, we all agree.

Uranus giggles, a planet so bold,
It knows secrets that we have missed.
With each twinkle, a story told,
As Saturn's rings swirl, we can't resist.

Galactic parties, a starry ball,
While meteors zip, giving us fright.
Together we laugh, in this vast hall,
Underneath the laughs of the starlit night.

The Pulse of the Starlit Night

Stars play hopscotch, don't you see?
With constellations marking the way.
They twinkle and wink, full of glee,
As we ponder what they might say.

Cosmic karaoke, oh what a dream,
Planets belt out tunes that are bizarre.
Neptune's got jazz, it's quite the theme,
While Venus croons under a glowing star.

A shooting star races, what a sight!
Making wishes is all the rage.
But don't get too serious tonight,
Just dance with the cosmos off the page.

In this galactic bazaar of fun,
Where laughter echoes in the sky.
Catch a comet--now wouldn't that be fun?
As we scribble our dreams, oh me, oh my!

Lost in the Universe's Embrace

On a flying carpet made of stardust,
We zoom through space, oh what a ride!
Finding odd socks, as we must,
In the galaxy's treasure, we confide.

The moon dips low, it whispers jokes,
While comets serve drinks from the sky.
Rocket raccoons play pranks like folks,
Leaving us laughing, as we fly by.

A black hole's a friend, or so they say,
It swallows our worries, our fears, our stress.
In the cosmic whirl, we laugh and sway,
Making memories we couldn't guess.

With every twinkle, a chuckle near,
As the universe pulls us in tight.
No answers found, but that's quite clear,
We revel in laughter through the night!

Celestial Pilgrimages

We take a trip on solar winds,
With satirical stars as our guides.
Through meteor showers, humor begins,
As planets grin, and starlight abides.

Venus made pancakes, what a feat!
While Jupiter's juggling, looking quite grand.
The universe smiles, can't be beat,
Cosmic cuisine's always at hand.

Black holes throw parties, don't be late,
With wormholes leading the funky way.
Interstellar dances, oh celebrate,
In this wild galaxy, we sway.

As we roam through the stellar expanse,
Every giggle is etched in the dark.
The universe winks, and it's all a chance,
For laughter to echo, and leave its mark.

Insights from the Sky

When I gaze up at the night,
The stars wink back at my plight.
They giggle at my silly dreams,
While plotting cosmic schemes.

A moonbeam whispers soft and low,
'Your pizza's late, just let it go.'
The constellations roll their eyes,
As I argue with the skies.

I try to read the twinkling hints,
But find only wild cosmic prints.
The universe shrugs, gives a grin,
Says, 'You've got it all within.'

Oh, how these stars seem to delight,
In my blunders, such a sight.
They laugh as I seek truths afar,
While they just float, a giant bazaar.

Celestial Beacons of Truth

Shooting stars race like they're late,
To meetings with their cosmic fate.
They seem to say, 'Just make a wish,'
Then laugh at my detached fish.

The planets dance their dizzy waltz,
While I ponder my own faults.
They tease me with their radiant glow,
'Just relax! Enjoy the show!'

A comet zooms by with a cheer,
'Your laundry's still in disarray, dear!'
I wave back at this heavenly jest,
'Thanks for reminding me, you're the best!'

As I stew in my earthly mess,
The galaxies laugh, I must confess.
Their giggles ripple through the night,
In this cosmic comedy of light.

Stories Written in the Night

The stars gather for a midnight chat,
About my woes, my patterned hat.
They snicker, 'What's wrong with your hair?'
As I try to make it all so fair.

Constellations spill their ancient lore,
Of mishaps and hang-ups from yore.
I'm just another tale they'll tell,
Along with Jupiter, oh so swell.

The night sky scribbles with delight,
Puns and jests wrapped up so tight.
Each twinkle is a laugh, no doubt,
As I scroll through my personal shout.

Oh, how the heavens love a quip,
They'll poke fun at my mental trip.
With every star, a giggle spreads,
As I drift off to slumber, sans my threads.

Astral Navigation of the Soul

With a map made of stars, I start to steer,
Through cosmic bumps and laughter's cheer.
The Milky Way's a road of joy,
Lighting paths like a whimsical toy.

I asked Orion for directions clear,
He chuckled, 'Just follow what you hold dear.'
As Venus winked just up ahead,
I stumbled on thoughts I left unsaid.

Galaxies turned their spinning wheels,
While I chased the zest that life reveals.
They laughed at my tangled route and twist,
Saying, 'Unplanned paths often bring bliss.'

So here I float, a cosmic tease,
In orbit 'round the joy, no need to freeze.
The universe gives a wink and grin,
As I embrace the fun I'm living in.

A Starry Canvas of Understanding

In the sky, I ask a question,
Do the stars have a suggestion?
They twinkle and giggle with glee,
"Maybe try not to spill your tea!"

I squint up at the shining bright,
Are they critiquing my outfit tonight?
With each sparkle, a wink and a tease,
"Buddy, just stick to the cheese!"

Is that a comet I see zoom by?
Or just my neighbor's flying pie?
I laugh at the wisdom they share,
If only I could join them up there!

So let's dance under this shining dome,
With cosmic giggles, we can roam,
For in the vastness, no stress to find,
Just don't forget your starry mind!

Reflections in Galactic Waters

Staring at the pond one night,
The stars winked back, oh what a sight!
"Is that you, or a firefly prank?"
They shimmered, not caring to rank!

Should I fish for wisdom from the deep?
Or simply let the universe sweep?
The frogs croak laughter from their throne,
"Just chill, dude, you're not alone!"

If fish can swim in starry streams,
Then surely they share cosmic dreams.
Each ripple a giggle, a tale to tell,
As I ponder, I'm under their spell!

So here's to the water, the stars, and me,
Hosting an intergalactic tea!
With marshmallows dancing on the waves,
We celebrate all our cosmic braves!

The Art of Cosmic Navigation

With my map of stars, I set to sail,
But wind and light keep me frail.
"Is that a planet or a pizza slice?"
Oh, why can't navigation be nice?

I tried to steer using the moon,
But it thumped like a very bad tune.
The meteors laughed, zooming past,
"This isn't a race, just have a blast!"

Constellations dance, swirling so bright,
Each one a guide in the shimmering night.
"You missed a turn—go back, go back!"
But who knew stars could be such a knack?

So I'll chart my course with a grin so wide,
Through cosmic chaos, I'll joyfully glide.
For every bump is a funny plot,
Navigating the space where laughter is hot!

Dreams Woven in Stardust

Every night I dream awake,
In a blanket of stars, for goodness' sake!
A squirrel with wings says, "Hey, take flight!"
While shooting stars steal my dish of delight!

I meet a bear who's learning to rhyme,
Dancing with aliens, having a good time.
"What do you want?" they cheer with glee,
"Just some laughter and maybe some tea!"

We spin in circles made of comet trails,
Trading our stories, our cosmic tales.
Each giggle a spark, igniting the night,
These dreams so funny, the stars just ignite!

So let's weave our dreams with laughter, my friend,
In the cosmic tapestry that'll never end.
For in this universe, where joy expands,
We're all simply stardust, in fun we stand!

A Celestial Choir of Answers

In the sky, a band of notes,
Winking suns and giggling goats.
The planets dance in silly ways,
Spinning tales of better days.

Stars twinkle like a child at play,
Whispering secrets, 'Come what may.'
Nebulas puff like cotton candy,
Who knew the universe was so handy?

The Cosmos' Hidden Narratives

Galaxy spin like a game of tag,
With comet trails that make you gag.
Black holes munch on space-time snacks,
While pyramids hide their prankster hacks.

Asteroids tumble with a laugh,
Creating chaos on their path.
Fill the void with quirky signs,
Telling jokes across the lines.

Embracing Celestial Paradoxes

A star can be both bright and dim,
As moons wear shades on a cosmic whim.
Gravity's pulling like an old friend,
Tugging at dreams that never end.

Saturn's rings a circus theme,
While Jupiter's storms just love to scream.
The universe quirks, it jumps and twirls,
Sporting mustaches and purple swirls.

Resilient Stars in the Night

Stars sometimes trip when they're on high,
Twinkle down like a wink or a sigh.
Galaxies giggle, they wink and whirl,
While black holes just eat this dance of swirl.

A cosmic laugh, a bumpy ride,
As meteors race, side by side.
In this vast and quirky sea,
The universe grins—come laugh with me!

Journeys Through Astral Legends

In the quiet night, I take a peek,
To find the secrets that the cosmos speak.
Aliens giggle at my clumsy fate,
As I trip on space rocks and contemplate.

The moon winks down, a mischievous friend,
Saying, "Hey, Earthling, you'll never transcend!"
Saturn's rings twist, a cosmic joke told,
As I try to catch stardust, bold and old.

Big comets fly by, they wave and tease,
While I'm tangled in cosmic unease.
"Keep moving, human, don't be so slow!"
But my space boots are stuck in a nebula's glow.

Yet in the chaos, a spark ignites,
In the laughter of stars, I find my sights.
Astral myths burst, like popcorn in flight,
And I dance through the cosmos, both silly and bright.

Stardust Chronicles

Up in the sky, where wishes collide,
A squirrel holds court on a comet with pride.
"Why chase your dreams?" he chuckles with glee,
"They're all in my pocket, just waiting for tea!"

Planets chuckle, as their orbits loop,
With folksy tunes from a cosmic soup.
"Grab a seat, sit tight, the show's about to start,
Who knew the universe had such a funny heart?"

Galaxies spin as I wave goodbye,
To the aliens laughing, oh my, oh my!
"Is that a UFO or just my bad hair?"
Socketed stars sound like they don't care!

In the stardust sprinkle, absurdity reigns,
Like a comet wearing glasses with chains.
With each giggle, a truth comes alive,
Comedy's proof that the cosmos can thrive!

The Heavens Hold Their Wisdom

A wise old star with a beard of light,
Tells me jokes as we dance through the night.
"Why did the planet break up with the sun?
It found someone cooler, who outshone the fun!"

Each constellation's like a quirky group,
Playing charades with a celestial troupe.
"Hey, Orion! Show us your best missing pants!"
While the Pleiades giggle, pointing at chance.

Jupiter's storms rave, making a mess,
"Come clean, dear Earth, you've got such a stress!"
But I break out a smile, ignoring the fuss,
For the cosmos is buzzing, just marvelous!

As the meteors race, they whisper and play,
Reminding me laughter won't fade away.
So I groove with the stars, their wisdom I find,
In the joyful chaos, I leave troubles behind!

Threads of Infinity

Little sparkles dance, wearing shiny shoes,
Picking up dreams like they're Monday's news.
The galaxies spin, and what do they see?
An Earthling tripping over a cup of green tea.

Threads of fate weave in comical swirls,
As Venus recites tongue twisters that twirl.
"Try saying 'supernova' five times fast,
You'll end up like comets, in a blast!"

The stars tap their feet, with laughter and cheer,
Saying, "Who knew mortals could outshine a sphere?"
Cosmic hiccups fill the space where I roam,
With echoes of giggles that feel like home.

So I follow their lead, this bright, crazy game,
Imitating suns, forgetting my name.
In this surreal circus, I find my delight,
Crafted by laughter, wrapped in starlight.

Dancing with Celestial Shadows

Twinkle twinkle, cosmic toes,
Dancing round where the stardust flows.
Asteroids swing, and comets prance,
Gravity forgot, in this vast expanse.

Galaxies giggle, what a sight,
Constellation costumes, oh so bright!
Moonbeams waltz on rings of ice,
Planets joke, oh isn't it nice?

Stars whisper secrets, giggles they share,
Space is the party, without a care.
Quasars laugh with a booming sound,
While black holes hide, where fun's not found.

A cosmic joke, a universal jest,
In this game of fate, we're all the best.
So dance with shadows, let cosmos lead,
In the orbit of laughter, we'll plant our seed.

Astral Letters of the Past

Once upon a time, in the great beyond,
Stars scrawled stories, a cosmic correspond.
Mailbox on Mars, letters take flight,
With jokes from Jupiter, oh what a sight!

Venus complained 'bout her lack of space,
While Saturn sent puns that embraced our grace.
The Milky Way giggled, 'twas all in good fun,
As moonbeams caught laughter, each race had to run.

A comet whizzed past, delivering cheer,
'Brought you some stardust, and maybe a tear.'
Yet wisdom floats in this humor-filled chat,
All letters enclosed with a cosmic fat cat!

So read what you will, with a smile or a grin,
These astral reports, where friendships begin.
For even the cosmos can teach us to jest,
In this boundless universe, humor's the best.

Infinite Questions Under a Shared Sky

Under the stars, we ponder and muse,
'What's the best snack for a Martian cruise?'
'Can UFOs cook, or is that just a myth?'
'What kind of shoes does an alien gift?'

Questions swirl like planets on a spin,
Why do they laugh with their green, toothy grin?
Is there a school where comets go learn?
Or do they just wing it, in twists and returns?

The sun chimes in with a bright shining jest,
'Go pick your favorite star, or you're just a guest!'
With answers that twinkle, so far yet so near,
We gather our questions, loud, proud, and sincere.

And maybe the truth, in its glittering guise,
Is found in these queries, 'neath infinite skies.
So dance with your thoughts, let them fly and whirr,
For shared laughter echoes, a cosmic stir.

Navigating the Nebula of Existence

In this fog of stars, I lost my way,
Tracking down answers, come what may.
Navigating through clouds, with a star map in hand,
Finding a giggle in dark cosmic land.

Asteroids bump, play tag with delight,
A supernova burst, oh what a sight!
With each twisty turn, I laugh at the chase,
While starlings chuckle, it's all a show race.

In the heart of the dust, I find my path bright,
Meteors whisper, 'Just enjoy the night!'
For every misstep, a joke's on display,
As I trip on halos, and float on bouquet.

The nebula giggles, it knows all my fears,
Yet dances with me, through the swirling years.
So I'll race through this void, with a grin and a cheer,
In a universe laughing, there's nothing to fear!

Ascendants of the Celestial Dreamers

In a world where comets tease,
A cat pays homage on its knees.
The planets giggle, stars will gleam,
While Earthlings shake their heads and scream.

Luna winks at the moody sun,
Mars tells jokes, oh what fun!
Asteroids dance like clumsy fools,
While we just bumble, breaking rules.

Nebulae swirl in a cosmic twirl,
As we spin on like a dizzy whirl.
Stargazers trip, fall flat on their backs,
Chasing dreams in galactic tracks.

So grab a friend and raise a toast,
To cosmic mysteries we love the most.
In the end, it's all a game,
The universe giggles, it's never the same!

Of Celestial Journeys and Earthly Roots

An owl took off to find its fate,
Wobbled in space, oh isn't that great?
Gravity giggled, gave it a shove,
As it asked the stars, 'Where's the love?'

Orion yawned, stretched and sighed,
'Scuse me, I'm just too starry-eyed.
Venus blinked, said 'You're quite bold,
But do watch out for asteroids, old!'

A rocket cat flew by with flair,
Chasing its tail through the cosmic air.
Earth's just a pitstop, that's a fact,
That cosmic traffic? What a distraction!

With friends in orbit, we joke and play,
Stargazing brings another ridiculous day.
Wear those space suits, let's take a loop,
In this stellar circus, we're all part of the troop!

The Star Map of Existence

Constellations scribble in cosmic fonts,
While meteors dash and make big haunts.
'Hey, where's the party?' stars start to shout,
On this map, you can't lose your route!

Saturn spins with its rings so wide,
Jupiter laughs, it's a cosmic slide.
Black holes whisper secrets, trying to tease,
As aliens giggle, 'Can we have some cheese?'

Starlight sparkles like cosmic sprinkles,
Shooting stars race, oh how it twinkles.
But who can really handle the flight,
When the Milky Way throws a pizza night?

So grab your telescope, let's take a look,
At the nailed-in destinies, just like a book.
Make some wishes while we joke and jest,
The universe is our grandest quest!

Chronicles of a Cosmic Traveler

With a suitcase packed, I took to the sky,
'What's over there?' asked a curious by.
The moon winked as I made my way,
Hitchhiking comets—what a weird day!

Space whales sing in a galactic choir,
While I try to find my interstellar attire.
Aliens giggle at my Earthly shoes,
'You call that fashion? You're bound to lose!'

So I danced with the stars, oh what a sight,
Fell on Mars, that was quite a fright!
From black holes to nebulae, I took it all in,
While the cosmos laughed at my silly grin.

Adventure calls, so I'll wave goodbye,
To the planets that wink and the stars that fly.
With stories to share at the edge of time,
I'll scribble my tale in a cosmic rhyme!

Starlit Secrets Unfold

Gazing up at twinkling lights,
I wonder what they think at nights.
Do they laugh at silly dreams we weave?
Or cheer us on as we believe?

I asked one star, 'Hey, don't you care?'
It winked at me, 'I'm busy, fair!'
So I wrote my wishes in the air,
Hoping it might just stop and stare.

The Milky Way's like cosmic jam,
A celestial bread with wacky spam.
I toast to stars that guide my quest,
They surely know how to jest!

So spin your dreams with stardust flair,
And dance about without a care.
For in this galaxy full of fun,
The universe is never done!

Celestial Riddles of Existence

In the sky, I see a quiz,
Is that a comet or just a fizz?
Shooting stars or just a plane?
Guessing wrong, it drives me insane!

Constellations tell a tale so grand,
With Gemini and Leo hand in hand.
Is that a bear or just a dog?
My mind gets lost in this cosmic fog!

I asked Orion, 'What's your game?'
He just smirked, 'I'm not to blame.'
The stars hold secrets, laugh or cry,
But all I see is pizza pie!

So grab your telescope, come and peek,
Join the riddle—the stars don't speak!
Their silence is cosmic, yet so sly,
Answering questions with a wink and sigh.

Echoes in the Cosmos

Echoes bounce from star to star,
Do they hear my wishes from afar?
Or laugh and say, 'Oh, what a goof!'
As I trip over my cosmic roof!

Whispers of comets, giggles of moons,
Tickling thoughts with other tunes.
What's that noise? Is it a joke?
Or just my dreams, a funny hoax?

A nebula shouts, 'Can't you see?',
We are all shining, wild and free!
So throw those worries to the skies,
And watch them twirl with joyous sighs!

The cosmos chuckles, swirls about,
Filling the heavens with giddy shout.
So let our thoughts dance in the light,
For laughter echoes through the night!

Navigating by Celestial Light

Under moonlight, I take my stand,
Trying to map this starry land.
North or south? I'm on the fence,
But the stars just giggle in suspense!

With my map of twinkles drawn,
I step outside at crack of dawn.
'Where's my guide?' I loudly plead,
But starlight's stubborn, laughs at my need.

A planet grins, 'Hey, just relax!'
While comet tail leaves funny tracks.
Steering my ship through space-time waves,
In this cosmic riddle, nobody saves!

So let's dance under this vast sky,
With starlight guiding, oh me, oh my!
For in this twinkling twist of fate,
The universe knows how to celebrate!

Orion's Silent Wisdom

In the sky, a hunter's bow,
With arrows aimed at hearts in woe.
When stars align and giggles start,
He whispers truths, but not to part.

His belt's a cinch for pants so tight,
With cosmic jokes that shine so bright.
If you listen close and take a peek,
You'll find he's just a real star geek.

He grins at planets, floats in glee,
While meteors craft a raucous spree.
So next time you feel lost or small,
Remember, Orion laughs at all.

When wishes fade and dreams may rust,
Just look above; in stars, we trust.
For cosmic giggles twinkle clear,
And in starlit nights, there's naught to fear.

When Planets Align

When planets dance in playful spins,
The cosmos dons its twinkling sins.
Venus winks, and Mars gives chase,
While Jupiter juggles in endless grace.

A galactic party with no invite,
Each starry guest feeling just right.
Saturn's rings, a hula-hoop night,
As comets sparkle, what a sight!

Galaxies swirl in a wobbly line,
As Uranus tells jokes, rather benign.
With laughter echoing through the void,
Even black holes can't get annoyed.

So when you see those planets prance,
Remember, it's all just cosmic chance.
In the sky, where fun is divine,
We learn that chaos can oft entwine.

Constellations of the Heart

In the night, love's shapes appear,
A heart from stars that's crystal clear.
With laughter stitched in every glance,
The universe throws a sweet romance.

Pisces giggles, with fish that flop,
While Scorpios dance and never stop.
Cancer hugs with glowing light,
As Leo roars with pure delight.

Each twinkling star, a secret shared,
In this galactic game, we dared.
With constellations mapping our fate,
The cosmos giggles, isn't it great?

So hold your dreams beneath the moon,
And let hearts sing a cosmic tune.
For in this universe, wild and bold,
Our starlit stories will be told.

The Night Sky's Promises

The night sky writes with starlit pens,
Sketching tales of amorous friends.
With every wink from the lunar face,
A promise wrapped in cosmic grace.

Shooting stars make wishes strong,
While constellations hum a joyful song.
As comets streak with tails so bright,
They giggle, saying, "We've got this night!"

The moon chuckles, a silvery clown,
As clouds drift softly, up and down.
In the universe's whimsical spree,
A promise waits for you and me.

So laugh with the stars, and feel the cheer,
For in the cosmos, there's naught to fear.
With every twinkle, our dreams ignite,
In the night sky's embrace, we feel just right.

Harvesting Light from the Night Sky

The moon is a giant disco ball,
Reflecting our hopes, both big and small.
Stars wink like friends who know the joke,
While we plow through dreams and cosmic smoke.

Comets dash by, with tails so bright,
Chasing our laughter, in the dead of night.
They stop for a sip of stardust tea,
And whisper, "Is the universe just you and me?"

Asteroids dance like they just got paid,
Spinning in circles, high in the shade.
While galaxies chuckle, "Did you hear that?"
As we chase our thinking, so silly and fat.

So look up high, don't miss the show,
With sparkles above, and ideas down low.
We'll gather the magic, a celestial spree,
Harvesting light, just you and me.

The Harmony of Starbound Journeys

Spaceships zoom past like fireflies,
Singing their tunes under velvet skies.
Each star a note, in a cosmic score,
While we're dancing on dreams, begging for more.

Planets are busy, with parties in tow,
Jupiter's moon just stole the show.
Mars in a bowtie, oh what a sight,
As Saturn spins records, all through the night.

Aliens giggle, in their own little way,
As they join our dance, on this playful array.
We're all starbound beings, lost in a trance,
Forget the worries and join the space dance.

So gather your friends, and hold them real tight,
Let's journey together, through starry delights.
In this harmony, we shimmer and sway,
Creating cosmic echoes that never decay.

Paintbrush of the Universe

With a brush made of stardust and dreams,
I'll paint the sky with ridiculous schemes.
Neon swirls of laughter and fun,
Creating a canvas, for everyone.

Stars giggle softly, like old friends do,
As I mix up the colors of red, green, and blue.
Clouds are my canvas, vast and divine,
And I'm the artist, oh what a line!

The sun yells, "Yo! Don't forget my glow!"
While the comets pass by, putting on a show.
Each twinkle a joke, each splash a rhyme,
As galaxies burst forth, lively and sublime.

So come grab a brush, let's make our mark,
With laughter and whimsy, we'll ignite the spark.
In this playful universe, we'll shine bright,
Painting the heavens with pure delight.

Galactic Echoes of the Heart

I sent a text to a star last night,
Asking for wisdom, to set things right.
But all I got back was an emoji smile,
I guess they're just busy, chasing the mile.

Nebulas whisper secrets, oh so sly,
"Don't take it so seriously, give it a try!"
They giggle like children, gas clouds in flight,
As they plot their next trick, under cosmic light.

Supernovas pop like confetti in air,
Celebrating with twirls, no worry or care.
The black holes are hungry, but they won't bite,
Just spinning in joy, all through the night.

So let's laugh with the stars, in this cosmic art,
For echoes of giggles reside in the heart.
In the galaxy's glow, we'll find our way,
With humor and light, come join the play!

An Astral Journey of Discovery

In the quiet night, I gaze above,
Stars twinkle like they've just found love.
Winks and giggles in the cosmic show,
Are they laughing at us? Well, maybe so.

Planets spinning like they're at a dance,
Mars forgot his steps – what a clumsy chance!
Saturn's rings are quite a sight,
Looks like jewelry for a starry night.

I ponder my fate in this vast embrace,
If only I could join this interstellar race.
But my spaceship's too small for a big launch,
Guess I'll just settle for a night on the couch.

So here's to the heavens, funny and bright,
Their cosmic jokes fill the dark with light.
Maybe tomorrow I'll shoot for the stars,
Or just take a nap – it can't be that far!

Luminescent Personas of the Sky

Oh look! There's Orion, with his hunter's pose,
Wielding distractions nobody knows.
His belt is a reminder not to lose style,
Even space cowboys can have a bright smile.

And there's silly Gemini, always in pairs,
Bickering like siblings on cosmic affairs.
They must be tired from all that debate,
Why not just chill? Relax, it's getting late!

A comet races by, waving at the Moon,
"Catch me if you can!" sings a starry tune.
With a trail of glitter, and gasps of surprise,
Even comets must get bored of their routines.

Yet up there they dance, without a care,
Creating star maps we can only stare.
With each shooting star, a wish may unfold,
But remember, dear friend, some wishes are bold!

Reflections in the Cosmic Mirror

Stargazing's a hobby for thinkers and dreamers,
But to them, I'm a comedian with cosmic schemers.
Oh, look! A constellation with its funny name,
Laughing at stories that never feel the same.

The Big Dipper's got a scoop, just look at it shine,
Pointing out people like they're fine wine.
"Gather 'round, folks! Time for the show,
Let me tell you tales from the great afterglow!"

Meanwhile, a meteor thinks it's a rockstar,
Falling through the night with its flamboyant car.
But all it finds is a dusty old cloud,
"Hey, not my crowd!" it shouts, shouting loud.

As I chuckle with stars, this cosmic delight,
I realize this journey is a circus at night.
With a wink and a nod, the galaxy giggles,
A dance of absurdity, for all us squiggles!

When Stars Align with Purpose

The stars are aligned, the horoscopes say,
But I can't find my socks, what a funny fray!
Mercury is retrograde, so they claim,
Is that why I lost my wallet? Oh, what a game!

Jupiter juggles its moons like a pro,
While Venus giggles, "Hey, don't steal the show!"
Mars shakes its fists, but with playful dread,
"Why can't we just all have a snack instead?"

As the moon pulls the tides with a grand old twist,
I wonder if under this glow, I'll be missed.
All these heavenly bodies, what's their grand aim?
To spice up my life with a little more fame?

So here we are, tumbling through space,
With starry best friends in a cosmic embrace.
If the universe's plan includes laughter and cheer,
Count me in, oh stars! Let's all have a beer!

A Symphony of Celestial Stories

Twinkling lights in the night,
Winking down with delight.
Stars gossip, oh what a sight,
Who knew they could be so bright?

The Big Dipper spins a yarn,
Of pizza parties on a farm.
Orion plays the cosmic guitar,
While comets dance, oh how bizarre!

Galaxies whisper secrets vague,
As planets juggle, doing a rave.
Supernovae burst in cheer,
"Did you hear? The moon drank beer!"

So let's raise our eyes in jest,
To cosmic shows, they're the best!
For every spark in the cloud,
Sings laughter, singing out loud!

Secrets of the Night Unfold

Once a star fell with a wish,
Said it dreamed of a swish.
"Catch me now," it started to plead,
But landed in a cosmic feed!

Constellations throw a dance,
As meteors take their chance.
"Hey, I'm shooting!" one exclaimed,
"Watch my skills," he proudly claimed!

The moon chuckled, glowing bright,
"Did you wear that hat tonight?"
To Venus, who blushed in blue,
"Let's throw a party! Just us two!"

Remember, when you gaze above,
The stars have quirks you'll love.
Each twinkle, giggle, spark of fun,
In this cosmic race, we've all won!

The Tapestry of the Universe

Once I saw a shooting star,
Said it just came from afar.
"I've been practicing my flip,
Next week I'll try a back-slip!"

Planets swirl like a grand parade,
While asteroids jostle, not afraid.
"Excuse me, star," one did shout,
"Move over, I'm coming out!"

Galaxies form a quirky line,
Singing songs of space and time.
"Every logo's got a flair,
Join our club—if you dare!"

So don't forget to look and see,
The cosmos hosts such jubilee.
In the chart of spirits so grand,
Laughter creates a merry band!

Patterns of Light in Darkness

In the dark, the stars have flair,
Twinkling tales they love to share.
"Did you hear? The sun's a clown!"
So said Orion in his gown.

Aliens, dressed in silver suits,
Dance beneath with groovy roots.
"Join us, Earthlings! Let's uplift,
The cosmos loves a good gift!"

Planets spinning like a wheel,
Comedic routines they can feel.
"Oops, I tripped on a moon beam!"
Making starlight's laughter stream.

So when you're filled with doubts and fears,
Look above and reshape cheers.
For even in the vast expanse,
The universe loves a playful dance!

Stardust Chronicles

In the sky, bright dots play,
A game of hide and seek each day.
I asked a star, 'What's the score?'
It winked and twinkled, then said, 'More!'

Cosmic giggles, gravity's tease,
I floated up with the greatest of ease.
What should I wear for this celestial ball?
My pajamas, of course! They fit me best of all!

Galaxies spin in a whirl of delight,
Planets dance wildly, twinkling so bright.
I tripped on a nebula, fumbled my shoe,
The cosmos just laughed, said 'That's what we do!'

Now I jot down this starry advice,
To ALWAYS wear socks that are fun and nice.
When in doubt, grab a starlit dessert,
For laughter and joy always come first!

Where the Milky Way Meets the Soul

Have you seen the moon's silly face?
It pulls all tides, but runs the race.
While stars all snicker from high above,
They bet on which comet falls in love.

A starry duo, waltzing in sync,
While others just bubble, they laugh and wink.
'What's the secret?' I asked with glee,
They pointed to chocolate and said, 'You see!'

Milky Way, with its creamy swirl,
Is the favorite drink of an interstellar girl.
I spilled it once—who knew? What a scene!
The black hole chuckled, 'You're a space-time bean!'

Shooting stars fall, but not with grace,
They instead ponder their cosmic place.
So if you're lost, just take a peek,
The universe will laugh, whisper, and speak.

Nightfall's Silent Confessions

When darkness falls, and stars make bets,
The moon spills secrets, no regrets.
'Confess your dreams to the cosmic waves,'
And hope the aliens don't call you knaves!

Twinkling wonders all line the sky,
With stardust wafting, we laugh and sigh.
A galaxy said, 'You're an earthly clown!'
I replied, 'Yes, but with a shiny crown!'

In the still of night, mysteries swirl,
I thought I heard a comet giggle and twirl.
'What's the meaning of this shining spree?'
'Just aim for the cosmos, and sippy your tea!'

Each twinkling light starts to snicker,
While black holes just loom, making things thicker.
Shooting stars dash with mirthful delight,
Remember, they're only here for the night!

Comets and the Heart's Journey

Comets zoom by, a flash and a dash,
With flaming tails—a spectacular splash!
I once tried to catch one, thought I could fly,
But ended up tangled in a space potato pie!

With every loop and every curl,
The universe spins in a whimsical whirl.
A comet chuckled, 'Just take it slow!'
I replied, 'That's hard when you're in a show!'

Stars keep a diary, you wouldn't believe,
Full of snickers and cosmic reprieves.
'I wrote a confession,' one star said with ease,
'But forgot to sign it—oops, oh geez!'

So if you hear laughter among the bright,
Know it's just comets with a joke in flight.
In the galaxy, we're all made of fun,
Dancing through space, where time can't outrun!

Celestial Reflections

When I gaze up at the night,
I see winks and cosmic bites.
Planets laughing as they twirl,
Stars are just a wink in this worldly swirl.

Comets racing, what a sight,
Like they're late for a galactic fight.
Constellations juggling, stars in capes,
Trying to figure out their glowing shapes.

Asteroids spin, thinking they're cool,
While meteors flash, like they just broke a rule.
Galaxies spiral, isn't it odd?
In the vastness, who's the cosmic god?

I asked a star for some sage advice,
It flickered back, "Be a little nice!"
So here I am, with my head in the clouds,
Hoping one day to join that starry crowd.

The Constellation's Whisper

The Big Dipper spills its drink,
While Orion's belt starts to wink.
Pisces swims in lazy loops,
Designing plans for starry snoops.

Shooting stars are such fast talkers,
Bragging about their length and squawkers.
Uranus giggles, "Hey, look at me!
I'm the butt of jokes around this galaxy!"

I asked the moon, "What's the game?"
It just chuckled, "Ain't it the same?"
Twinkling stars gave me a nudge,
"We're just here to maintain a grudge."

So I dance beneath this twinkling dome,
With starlight whispers, I feel at home.
Gravity keeps my feet on the ground,
But in my dreams, I'm a starship bound!

Cosmic Scripts Unveiled

Galaxies write with glittery ink,
Scripted secrets that make you think.
Supernovae burst in fits of glee,
Making space like a cosmic spree.

Black holes hiding their silly grins,
Swallowing comets like they're kin.
Quasars giggle with a vibrant light,
Creating tales of a starry night.

Little planets play tag in a rush,
Their orbits spinning in a playful hush.
While aliens laugh from afar,
"Why don't they just drive a space car?"

Oh, the universe has jokes to tell,
In every star, there's a laugh so swell.
So when you're lost and needing a map,
Look up above and just enjoy the clap.

Night's Eternal Guidance

The night sky is a crazy show,
With stars that dance and planets that glow.
I asked a Viking where to go,
He just shrugged, said, "Follow the glow!"

The Milky Way spills secrets wide,
With enough sparkle to overtake your pride.
Constellations giggle with mischief bright,
Chasing each other until the dawn's light.

In this cosmic circus, laughter's abound,
Each celestial body, a jester found.
Saturn's rings are the funniest thing,
Like flashy bling, they jingle and sing.

So join the twirl in this universe vast,
With cosmic clowns, make shadows cast.
For in the night, under celestial larks,
We find out joy is written in sparks.

Echoes of the Astral Realm

In the night sky, I look up high,
Where fish swim through cosmic fry.
Planets dance, a wobbly jive,
In a galaxy buzzing with bees and hives.

Shooting stars, they wink and tease,
Maybe they'll grant me light-hearted ease.
I scoff at fate, with a giggle or two,
For Jupiter knows I'm quirky and true.

Comets blare like an out-of-tune band,
Outrageous chaos, isn't it grand?
While aliens chuckle at our earthly plight,
I'd invite them for tea, and dance through the night.

So here's to the cosmos, full of jest,
Where fortunes hang out, like a cosmic fest.
Among twinkling lights, I'll prance and I'll play,
In a universe laughing, come what may!

Time Travel Through Celestial Gates

Hop on a starship, let's make a dash,
Fly back in time, can we swim with the brash?
Dinosaurs chuckle, "What's that on our back?"
While we attempt to ride them, what a knack!

Wormholes swirling, they tickle our toes,
Through history's pages, past giggles it goes.
Imagine the chats with kings and their maids,
While they sip their tea, we toss them our trades.

From flappers to fables, we shimmy and sway,
A hundred years later, it's still "What'll we say?"
In the time warp, I trip on my shoe,
And land in a world where absurdity grew.

So onward we zoom, through mischief and cheer,
Each paradox dancing, for all to hear.
With cosmic giggles, we'll frolic and spin,
For through clever mishaps, who knows where we've been?

Threads of Destiny in the Cosmos

Woven in stardust, threads of the bold,
With a needle of dreams, let the fables unfold.
I stitched a laugh, then danced with a grin,
As the fabric of cosmos embraced my kin.

Galaxies twirl, while I tripped on a seam,
Creating a ruckus, you'd think it's a dream.
In the patterns of fate, absurdities flare,
Where chaos and giggles float freely in air.

Constellations scoff, "Do we really align?"
While I poke the bear, are we joking the divine?
A tapestry woven with mischief and glee,
As we spin in a whirl with the cosmic decree.

So let's thread our sorrows with humor so bright,
Each stitch a reminder to laugh at our plight.
In the cosmos, we frolic, weaving tales so divine,
As echoes of destiny interlace and entwine.

The Poet's Guide to the Universe

Welcome, dear traveler, to the cosmic stage,
Where the sun scribbles poems on a galactic page.
With quips from the moon and snickers from Mars,
We pen our adventures among shooting stars.

"Never take life too seriously," chuckles the sun,
"Just make sure you laugh; it's much more fun!"
The comets chime in, with tails all aglow,
As we draft cosmic verses, without a woe.

Planets provide prompts, like "write us a tale,"
While asteroids crash, humor's never too frail.
In this universe vast, where chaos runs free,
Let's scribble some laughter, just you and me!

So grab your quill with starlit delight,
As we scribe our adventures in endless flight.
With humor as our guide, let's dance and create,
In the world of the cosmos, no room for fate.

www.ingramcontent.com/pod-product-compliance
Lightning Source LLC
Chambersburg PA
CBHW072141200426
43209CB00051B/239